States

MARYLAND

by Angie Swanson

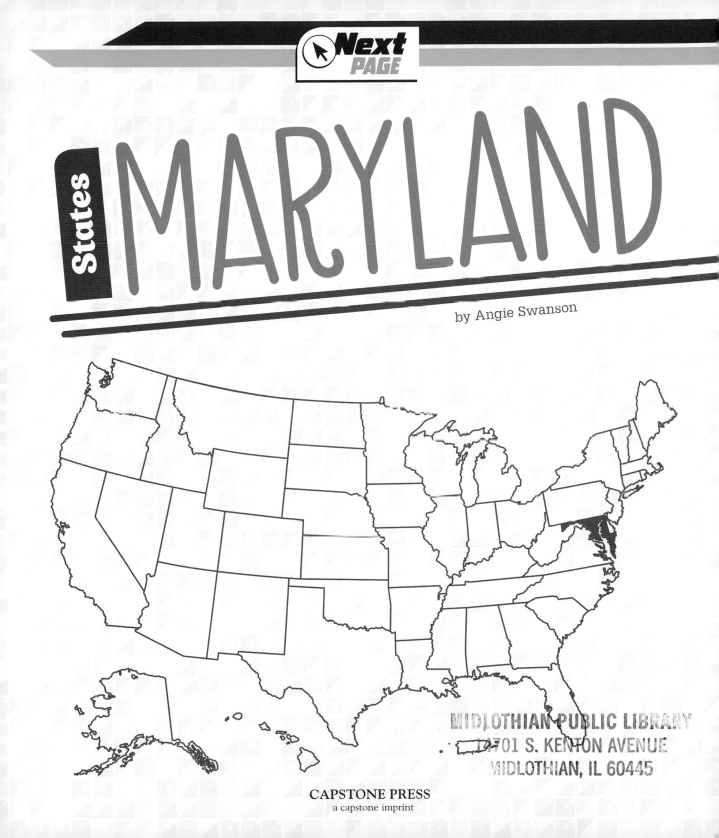

CAPSTONE PRESS
a capstone imprint

Next Page Books are published by Capstone Press,
1710 Roe Crest Drive, North Mankato, Minnesota 56003
www.mycapstone.com

Library of Congress Cataloging-in-Publication Data
Cataloging-in-publication information is on file with the Library of
Congress.
ISBN 978-1-5157-0407-2 (library binding)
ISBN 978-1-5157-0466-9 (paperback)
ISBN 978-1-5157-0518-5 (ebook PDF)

Editorial Credits
Jaclyn Jaycox, editor; Richard Korab and Katy LaVigne, designers;
Morgan Walters, media researcher; Laura Manthe, production specialist

Photo Credits
AP Images: ASSOCIATED PRESS, 28; Capstone Press: Angi Gahler,
map 4, 7; Dreamstime: Ken Cole, bottom left 21; Getty Images:
UniversalImagesGroup, 25; iStockphoto: EyeJoy, 9; Library of Congress:
Library of Congress Prints and Photographs Division Washington, D.C.,
27, 29, Prints and Photographs Division/Alexander Gardner, top 18,
Prints and Photographs Division/H. B. Lindsley, bottom 18, Prints and
Photographs Division/U.S. News & World Report Magazine Photograph
Collection/Thomas J. O'Halloran, middle 18; Newscom: Oliver Berg/dpa/
picture-alliance/New, top 19; North Wind Picture Archives, 26; One Mile
Up, Inc., flag, seal 23; Shutterstock: Action Sports Photography, bottom
24, Al Mueller, bottom left 20, Andrei Medvedev, 15, Chris Parypa
Photography, 6, 16, cvm, top right 20, Everett Historical, 12, Gerald
A. DeBoer, bottom right 20, Jaochainoi, top 24, Jay Ondreicka, middle
left 21, Jon Bilous, 5, 7, bottom left 8, Lissandra Melo, 17, Lone Wolf
Photography, bottom right 8, Lovell, middle right 21, mj007, bottom
right 21, Nagel Photography, 13, Oleksiy Naumov, bottom 19, Pete
Hoffman, 11, Richard Thornton, 14, s_bukley, middle 19, Sean Pavone,
cover, Vera Zinkova, top left 21, Wendy Farrington, 10, Zuzule, top
right 21; Wikimedia: Jyamuca, top left 20

All design elements by Shutterstock

Printed and bound in China.
0316/CA21600187
012016   009436F16

TABLE OF CONTENTS

Want to take your research further? Ask your librarian if your school subscribes to PebbleGo Next. If so, when you see this, helpful symbol 🖱 throughout the book, log onto www.pebblegonext.com for bonus downloads and information.

LOCATION

Maryland is a small mid-Atlantic state. Pennsylvania borders Maryland to the north. Both Delaware and the Atlantic Ocean lie on Maryland's eastern border. Virginia is to the south, and West Virginia borders Maryland to the southwest and west. Washington, D.C. is located between Maryland and Virginia. The nation's capital was once a part of Maryland. Annapolis is the state's capital. Baltimore is Maryland's largest city, followed by Frederick and Rockville.

PebbleGo Next Bonus!
To print and label
your own map, go to
www.pebblegonext.com
and search keywords:
MD MAP

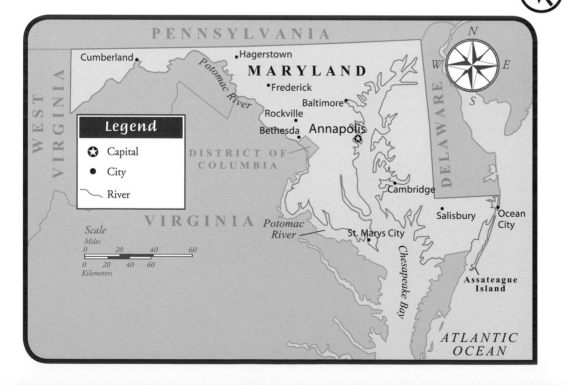

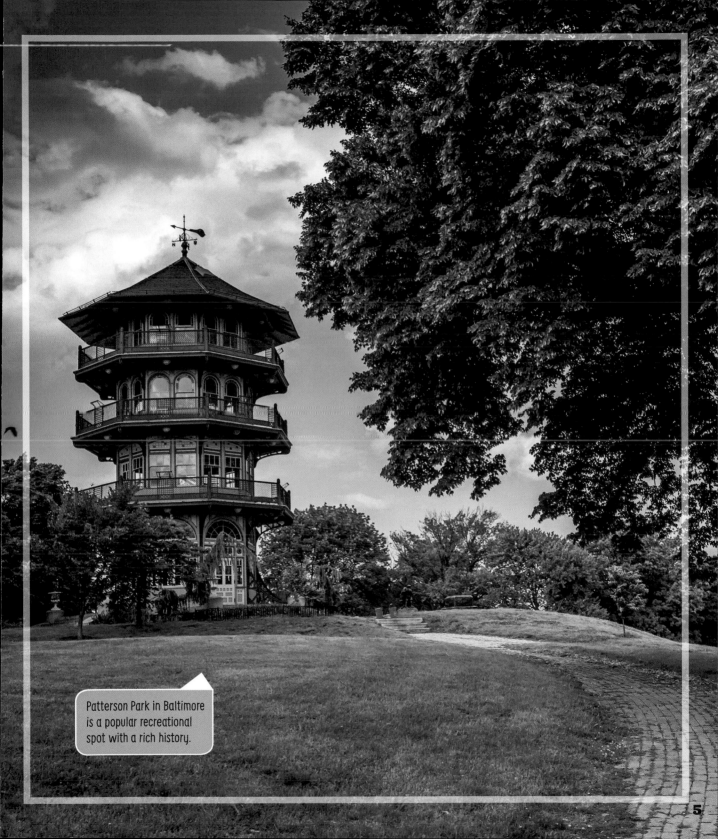

Patterson Park in Baltimore is a popular recreational spot with a rich history.

GEOGRAPHY

Maryland is a coastal state. Much of Maryland's coastline lies along Chesapeake Bay. Chesapeake Bay is the largest ocean bay in the United States. The state also has 30 miles (48 kilometers) of coast along the Atlantic Ocean. Assateague Island is located offshore. This island belongs to both Maryland and Virginia.

Maryland also has many rolling hills, valleys, and mountains. The mountainous Appalachian Plateau rises in the far western area of the state. Backbone Mountain, the state's highest point, stands 3,360 feet (1,024 meters) above sea level. Maryland has no natural lakes, but dams have created lakes and reservoirs.

PebbleGo Next Bonus!
To watch a video about Lexington Market, go to www.pebblegonext.com and search keywords:

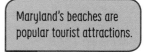

MD VIDEO

Maryland's beaches are popular tourist attractions.

The Chesapeake Bay is about 200 miles (320 km) long. It is the largest estuary in the United States.

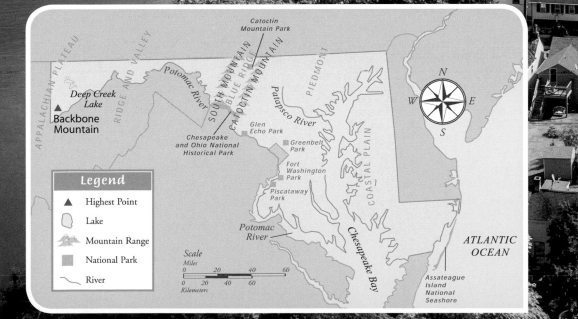

APPALACHIAN PLATEAU

RIDGE AND VALLEY

SOUTH MOUNTAIN

BLUE RIDGE

CATOCTIN MOUNTAIN

PIEDMONT

COASTAL PLAIN

Catoctin Mountain Park

Potomac River

Deep Creek Lake

Backbone Mountain

Chesapeake and Ohio National Historical Park

Glen Echo Park

Patapsco River

Greenbelt Park

Fort Washington Park

Piscataway Park

Potomac River

Chesapeake Bay

ATLANTIC OCEAN

Assateague Island National Seashore

N
W E
S

Legend

▲	Highest Point
⬭	Lake
⛰	Mountain Range
◼	National Park
∿	River

Scale
Miles
0   20   40   60
0   20 40   60
Kilometers

WEATHER

Maryland has mostly hot, humid summers and cool winters. The average summer temperature in Maryland is 73 degrees Fahrenheit (23 degrees Celsius). During the winter Maryland's average temperature is 34°F (1°C).

Average High and Low Temperatures (Annapolis, MD)

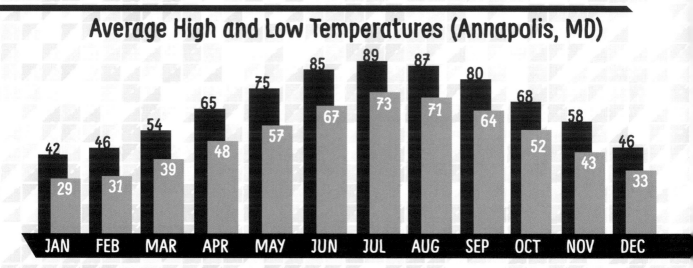

JAN	FEB	MAR	APR	MAY	JUN	JUL	AUG	SEP	OCT	NOV	DEC
42	46	54	65	75	85	89	87	80	68	58	46
29	31	39	48	57	67	73	71	64	52	43	33

LANDMARKS

Fort McHenry National Monument

During the War of 1812, the British attacked Fort McHenry in Baltimore. The Americans successfully defended the fort. Francis Scott Key watched the battle, which inspired him to write "The Star-Spangled Banner." Thousands of people visit the site each year.

Assateague Island

Wild ponies have roamed Assateague Island for more than 200 years. Two herds of wild ponies now live on the 37-mile- (60-km-) long island. Visitors to the island may see the ponies roaming the beaches, roadways, campgrounds, and marsh areas. No one is quite sure how the wild ponies came to the island.

Antietam National Battlefield

The Civil War Battle of Antietam was the bloodiest one-day battle in American history. About 23,000 soldiers were killed, wounded, or missing after the battle on September 17, 1862. The battle took place in Sharpsburg in northwestern Maryland. Visitors can see exhibits about the battle and the Civil War.

HISTORY AND GOVERNMENT

Lord Baltimore was the first proprietor of the Maryland colony.

Around 1200 American Indians built villages in Maryland. In 1631 Englishman William Claiborne built a trading post on Kent Island. In 1632 England's King Charles I promised George Calvert, also known as Lord Baltimore, a grant of land. His son, Leonard Calvert, led a group to Maryland in 1634 and established a colony. During the 1700s Maryland and Pennsylvania argued over state borders. Between 1763 and 1767, Englishmen Charles Mason and Jeremiah Dixon created a boundary line later known as the Mason-Dixon Line.

Maryland colonists fought in the American Revolution against Great Britain. The colonists won the war in 1783, and Maryland became the seventh state on April 28, 1788.

Maryland's government has three branches. The governor heads the executive branch. The legislative branch is called the General Assembly. It has two parts, the 47-member Senate and the 141-member House of Delegates. The court system makes up the judicial branch.

Maryland's state capitol building is located in Annapolis.

INDUSTRY

Milk, eggs, and other livestock products are Maryland's major farm products. Apples, peaches, pears, plums, and cherries are grown in western Maryland. The climate on the eastern shore is ideal for growing peaches, strawberries, and watermelons.

Fishing adds to the state's economy. The waters of the Chesapeake Bay provide crabs, oysters, and fish.

Maryland's natural harbor on the Chesapeake Bay allows ships to carry products to other states and countries. Baltimore is one of the major ports of the United States.

Sightseeing cruises are popular among tourists.

Products manufactured in the state include chemicals, metals, industrial machinery, and navigation equipment.

Sparrows Point is a major shipbuilding and repair center. Fishing boats and other small craft are built and repaired at boatyards throughout the Chesapeake Bay area.

The National Aquarium in Baltimore is the nation's first aquarium.

POPULATION

Just more than half of Maryland's population is white. Waves of immigrants came to Maryland from Europe during the 1700s and 1800s. Today members of many ethnic groups live in Maryland. Maryland's early settlers came from England. People from Germany and Ireland arrived later. Others came from Russia, Poland, Italy, and Greece.

Today almost 30 percent of Marylanders are African-Americans. Some African-Americans are descendants of southern slaves. In the 1800s many former slaves found safety in Maryland.

Population by Ethnicity

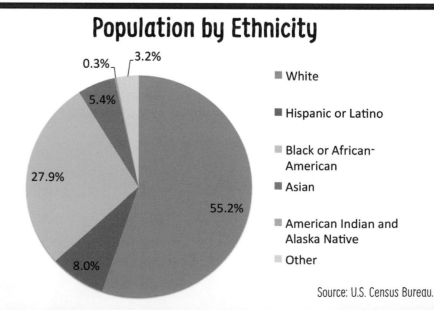

- White
- Hispanic or Latino
- Black or African-American
- Asian
- American Indian and Alaska Native
- Other

0.3%
3.2%
5.4%
27.9%
55.2%
8.0%

Source: U.S. Census Bureau.

The populations of other ethnic groups are growing in Maryland. Hispanics make up more than 8 percent of the state's population. That's double what it was in 2000. More than 5 percent of Marylanders are Asian. That's up from 4 percent in 2000.

FAMOUS PEOPLE

John Wilkes Booth (1838–1865) killed President Abraham Lincoln on April 14, 1865. He was born near Bel Air.

Thurgood Marshall (1908–1993) was the first African-American justice of the Supreme Court of the United States. He was born in Baltimore.

Harriet Tubman (1820–1913) was a former slave who helped many slaves escape to freedom. She was born in Dorchester County.

Jeff Kinney (1971–) is an author and cartoonist who created the *Diary of a Wimpy Kid* children's book series, which has sold more than 50 million copies worldwide. He grew up in Fort Washington.

Michael Phelps (1985–) is an Olympic swimmer. Phelps won 22 medals, 18 of them gold, in three Olympic Games. He was born in Baltimore.

Kevin Durant (1988–) is a three-time NBA All-Star and three-time NBA scoring champion for the Oklahoma City Thunder. He was born in Suitland.

STATE SYMBOLS

white oak

black-eyed Susan

Baltimore oriole

Baltimore checkerspot butterfly

PebbleGo Next Bonus! To make a dessert using Maryland's state drink, go to www.pebblegonext.com and search keywords: **MD RECIPE**

Cat

calico cat

Dog

Chesapeake Bay retriever

Reptile

diamondback terrapin

Sport

jousting

Boat

skipjack

Crustacean

Maryland blue crab

MINING PRODUCTS

coal, limestone, portland cement

MANUFACTURED GOODS

chemicals, computer and electronic products, food and beverage products

FARM PRODUCTS

chickens, corn, dairy products, soybeans, greenhouse products, fruit

PROFESSIONAL SPORTS TEAMS

Baltimore Orioles (MLB)
Baltimore Ravens (NFL)

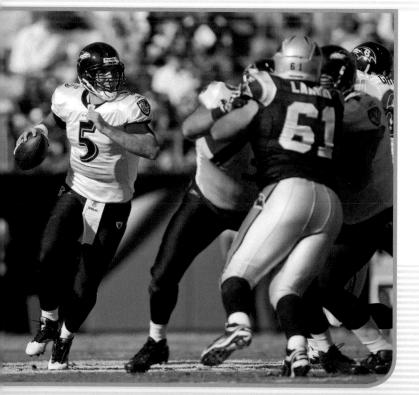

PebbleGo Next Bonus! To learn the lyrics to the state song, go to **www.pebblegonext.com** and search keywords:
MD SONG

MARYLAND TIMELINE

CIRCA 1200
American Indians begin to build villages in what is now Maryland.

EARLY 1600s
Settlers in Virginia travel to Maryland to trade with American Indians.

1608
Captain John Smith of the Jamestown colony in Virginia explores the Chesapeake Bay area.

1620
The Pilgrims establish a colony in the New World in present-day Massachusetts.

1632
King Charles I gives land in Maryland to George Calvert.

1634 — Leonard Calvert leads a group of settlers to Maryland on the ships *Ark* and *Dove*, settlers found St. Mary's City.

1692 — King William of England takes control of the colony.

1715 — The Calverts take back control of the colony.

1775–1783 — American colonists fight against the British in the Revolutionary War.

1788 — Maryland becomes the seventh state on April 28.

1791 — Maryland donates land for the new capital, Washington, D.C.

 **1814** During the War of 1812 (1812–1815), British soldiers burn Washington, D.C., and bomb Fort McHenry in Baltimore; Francis Scott Key writes "The Star-Spangled Banner."

 **1845** The U.S. Naval Academy opens in Annapolis.

 **1861–1865** The Union and the Confederacy fight the Civil War; Maryland remains in the Union, but a large number of Marylanders fight for the Confederacy.

 **1862** Union and Confederate troops fight the Battle of Antietam in Sharpsburg on September 17. It is the first battle of the Civil War fought in the North. More American lives are lost on this day than in any other in American military history.

 **1867** The present Maryland state constitution is adopted.

1914–1918 World War I is fought; the United States enters the war in 1917.

1939–1945 World War II is fought; the United States enters the war in 1941.

 **1952** The Chesapeake Bay Bridge opens on July 30. The bridge provides an important traffic link between Washington, D.C., and eastern Maryland and Delaware.

 **1967** Thurgood Marshall of Baltimore becomes the first African-American justice of the Supreme Court.

1980 Baltimore opens Haborplace, a marketplace located downtown. Shops there sell merchandise related to Baltimore.

2002 A thunderstorm takes down Maryland's 450-year-old Wye Oak tree in Wye Mills.

2011 The Messenger spacecraft, built at the John Hopkins University Applied Physics Laboratory in Laurel, becomes the first satellite to orbit Mercury.

2012 At the end of October, Hurricane Sandy hits Maryland and causes widespread damage there and in the entire northeast region.

2015 Maryland's ability to use solar power as an energy source increases by 174 percent—breaking the state's record!

Glossary

boundary *(BOUN-duh-ree)*—a border that separates one area from another

estuary *(ESS-chu-er-ee)*—the wide part of a river where it joins a sea

ethnicity *(ETH-niss-ih-tee)*—a group of people who share the same physical features, beliefs, and backgrounds

executive *(ig-ZE-kyuh-tiv)*—the branch of government that makes sure laws are followed

industry *(IN-duh-stree)*—a business which produces a product or provides a service

legislature *(LEJ-iss-lay-chur)*—a group of elected officials who have the power to make or change laws for a country or state

limestone *(LIME-stohn)*—a hard rock formed from the remains of ancient sea creatures

marsh *(MARSH)*—an area of wet, low land usually covered in grasses and low plants

plateau *(pla-TOH)*—an area of high, flat land

region *(REE-juhn)*—a large area

sea level *(SEE LEV-uhl)*—the average level of the surface of the ocean, used as a starting point from which to measure the height or depth of any place

Read More

Ganeri, Anita. *United States of America: A Benjamin Blog and His Inquisitive Dog Guide.* Country Guides. Chicago: Heinemann Raintree, 2015.

Otfinoski, Steven. *Maryland.* It's My State! New York: Cavendish Square Publishing, 2015.

Yasuda, Anita. *What's Great About Maryland?* Our Great States. Minneapolis: Lerner Publications, 2016.

Internet Sites

FactHound offers a safe, fun way to find Internet sites related to this book. All of the sites on FactHound have been researched by our staff.

Here's all you do:

Visit *www.facthound.com*

Type in this code: 9781515704072

 Check out projects, games and lots more at
www.capstonekids.com

Critical Thinking Using the Common Core

1. Maryland borrows its state motto from the Calvert family. What does the motto translate to in English? (Key Ideas and Details)

2. Maryland's coastline is along the Chesapeake Bay, the largest ocean bay in the United States. Explain how being located on the bay affects Maryland's industry. (Integration of Knowledge and Ideas)

3. The Appalachian Plateau is found in western Maryland. What is a plateau? Hint: Use the glossary for help. (Craft and Structure)

Index